YOUR KNOWLEDGE HAS VALUE

- We will publish your bachelor's and
  master's thesis, essays and papers

- Your own eBook and book -
  sold worldwide in all relevant shops

- Earn money with each sale

Upload your text at www.GRIN.com
and publish for free

Bibliographic information published by the German National Library:

The German National Library lists this publication in the National Bibliography; detailed bibliographic data are available on the Internet at http://dnb.dnb.de .

Cover image: pixabay.com

Imprint:

Copyright © 2019 GRIN Verlag
Print and binding: Books on Demand GmbH, Norderstedt Germany
ISBN: 9783346041975

This book at GRIN:

https://www.grin.com/document/504416

Mark Strutzenberger

The cryptocurrency Bitcoin. Its history, functional principles, security and economic aspects

GRIN Verlag

GRIN - Your knowledge has value

Since its foundation in 1998, GRIN has specialized in publishing academic texts by students, college teachers and other academics as e-book and printed book. The website www.grin.com is an ideal platform for presenting term papers, final papers, scientific essays, dissertations and specialist books.

Visit us on the internet:

http://www.grin.com/

http://www.facebook.com/grincom

http://www.twitter.com/grin_com

The cryptocurrency Bitcoin.
Its history, functional principles,
security and economic aspects

Mark Strutzenberger

Updated, English Version
Translated by Elena Zakharova

Abstract

This paper deals with the digital online currency Bitcoin, which is based on a decentralised system in which all users are equal, and there is no monopoly power. The currency allows one to conduct anonymous international transactions free of charge and in a split second. The system has potential not only as a store of value, but also as a means of payment. Due to the deflationary character caused by a limited money supply, a long-term increase in value can be expected. This paper describes risks and opportunities, as well as the way how this relatively new development works. Also, particular emphasis was placed on the security of the currency while using and how this can be improved. The main focus is on how the cryptocurrency was developed and who initiated it. Bitcoins are not stored and sent in a traditional way, but are incorporated into a collective memory by users themselves during the money creation process. All transactions are stored in the memory and, since it is publicly accessible, the system offers great transparency despite its anonymity.

Table of Contents

1. Introduction

Bitcoin was created in order to obviate traditional monetary policy. It and other similar currencies are collectively known as cryptocurrencies. The name bitcoin is a neologism and it derives from the word for the data unit, 'bit', and 'coin'. It has been equipped with functions that serve as a store of value as well as a medium of money transfer. It works via software commonly called a client or wallet. It creates a public and a private key. A public key functions as a bank account number and a private key fulfils a function similar to an online banking PIN number and also serves as a signature. Distinctive features of bitcoin provide protection against counterfeit coins and its decentralised structure which means the authorities do not have control over it. One of the most important characteristics is a facility for cost-effective transactions.[1]

By using mining software, a group of people called miners search for bitcoins in the blockchain. It works as follows: a computer processes transactions given its provided computational power. While the program on the PC is solving a complex computational problem, it can find a block in which transactions are stored. The solution called a hash value contains parts of a previous block so that it produces a string. As a result, blocks form a chain known as a blockchain, which represents the course of all transactions. The hash values of the previous blocks lay the basis for a new block. If a miner mines a block successfully, he obtains a block reward, new bitcoins which are awarded to the miner for conducting transactions. Thus, new bitcoins are generated. At the same time, they verify and store in the new block all money transfers which have happened since the last block.[2]

The objectives of this paper are to examine the functionality, risks, potential and history of bitcoin.

---

[1] Cf. Teich, Kai: Bitcoin Millionäre. Satoshi's Erben packen aus. Norderstedt: BoD – Books on Demand 2013, p.9f
[2] Cf. Ibid.

5

2. Functionality and Technology

The system is decentralised and therefore is a purely peer-to-peer network. Thus, money is transferred to without a third party involved. Moreover, the currency is deflationary, which means that the number of coins produced is limited to 21 million. Bitcoins can be divided up to the eighth decimal place; the smallest unit the currency is called a Satoshi. Satoshi are generated by users through complex calculations which are used for transaction processing as well.[3]

Since the network is unstructured, each unit can be removed without affecting the functionality of the network. Messages are sent in the network as quickly as possible using a flooding algorithm. The principle of the algorithm is that every recipient of a message passes it on to all known addresses except for the sender until everybody has received the information.[4]

The system combines the electronic transferability of bank money with the anonymity of cash. Transactions are stored in the blockchain. All transactions can be conducted internationally, not revocable and unable to be forged due to asymmetric key. Furthermore, they are free of charge or just a very small amount is charged.[5]

The structure of the network is similar to a global collective accounting system, so it is impossible to forge or to duplicate bitcoins unless a person or an organisation were in possession of a greater amount of computational power. All clients, which are user accounts, are visible in the network and are able to transfer money to other bitcoin addresses. Addresses own a public digital key that is used for a transfer of bitcoins; a private digital key is necessary for their receipt.[6]

2.1 Wallets, Addresses and Clients

Every user who deploys a connected client software owns one or several wallets, which are similar to real wallets; however, only keys are stored in them, not bitcoins. The client software calculates the account balance from credits and debits. Bitcoin addresses own one private and one public key which are mathematically compatible.

[3] Cf. Kerscher, Daniel: Handbuch der digitalen Währungen. Bitcoin, Litecoin und 150 weitere Kryptowährungen im Überblick. Dingolfing: Kemacon UG 2014, p.94ff
[4] Cf. Mölleken, Dirk: Bitcoin Geld ohne Banken – ist das möglich? Diploma theses. Diplomica Verlag GmbH Hamburg 2012, p.28ff
[5] Cf. ibid, p.21ff
[6] Cf. Cherek, Oliver: Bitcoin Risiken und Chancen einer digitalen Währung. Bachelor thesis. Nordersted: GRIN Verlag 2014, p.15ff

If transactions with mismatched keys are submitted, they will not be verified and processed by clients. The blockchain functions as a database in which every transaction is stored and visible to everyone.[7]

A client is a computer program, the term is usually used as a synonym for wallet. The distinction between them is that one client can possess several wallets. However, one wallet can contain any number of addresses. Some of them can be created automatically others added manually. Generally, the import of addresses which have been by other wallets is facilitated with the help of both keys.[8]

First of all, it should be decided how the keys will be stored. There are a number of different types of cryptocurrency wallets such as paper wallet, mind wallet, cold wallet, and software and hardware wallets.

2.1.1 Soft Wallets

Unlike hard wallets, which are physical special devices, soft wallets are programs installed on a computer with internet access. Thus, different clients should be taken into consideration.

2.1.1.1 Full Node Clients

A full node client is a program which stores the entire blockchain on a computer. At present, 198 gigabytes of memory space are needed to file it (Update 11/2018). This type of client requires high-speed internet as the blockchain is updated every 10 minutes. One of the advantages of full note clients is that there is no need to trust the third party and no infringement is possible. Moreover, the program supports the entire network, and it checks and validates transactions. As for verification, it is irrelevant who owns a sender or recipient address because a solution to a mathematical problem is whether correct and verified or incorrect and rejected. The generated copy of the network creates another backup that complicates manipulation attempts.[9]

---

[7] Cf. Platzer, Joerg: Bitcoin kurz & gut. Banking ohne Banken. Cologne: O'reilly 2014, p.18f
[8] Cf. Ibid, p.27ff
[9] Cf. Ibid.

2.1.1.2 Lite Clients

The functionality of a lite client resembles strongly that of a full node client. However, the required memory space is reduced by compression of the above-mentioned three-digit gigabyte number to a one-digit figure.[10]

2.1.1.3 SPV Clients

Simplified payment verification, or SPV, describes a type of client that does not download and update the entire blockchain. By using an algorithm, which functions like a filter, the SPV selects and stores the entries that are relevant to the management of private addresses.[11]

2.1.1.4 Server-dependent (Thin) Clients

Server-dependent clients, or thin clients, do not possesses a local copy of the blockchain, they use a blockchain stored by their provider instead. It is necessary to ensure that the software was published using open source as it makes infringement by a third party less likely. Furthermore, it must be kept in mind that the keys are stored locally and not in a network. All of this applies to the Electrum clients. One of the advantages of a thin client is its high readiness of use. On the other hand, downloading the entire blockchain takes several hours. The process might take days if the connection is slow.[12]

2.1.1.5 Web Wallets

Online wallets are not a software application, but rather websites in a web browser. The bitcoins are managed by the use of cloud systems. This allows the user to store data online as well as to access them from any device. Nevertheless, one should avoid this type of wallets, except for testing a system with a few euros or using it as a temporary solution. The reason is that there might be serious security problems, and third parties might control and manipulate the data.[13]

2.1.1.6 In-browser Clients

In-browser clients are a state-of-the-art development. They serve to make online payment fast and efficient by using a browser plug-in. The keys are stored locally, and

---

[10] Cf. Dr. Hosp, Julian: Kryptowährungen Bitcoin, Etherium, Blockchain, ICOs & Co. Einfach erklärt. 2nd edition. Munich: FinanzBuch Verlag 2018, p.86
[11] Cf. Platzer, 2014, p.28f
[12] Cf. Ibid, p.29f
[13] Cf. Ibid, p. 30f

the system is based on the open source concept. This means that its source code is public and discretionary. Moreover, it is possible to secure keys with a backup.[14]

2.1.2 Hard Wallets

Another new development is one type of a highly secured wallet. One stores the keys on a small single-purpose computer, which serves just this purpose. The key on the device is used to sign transactions that have been made in an online or a local wallet. As the keys are always placed on the device, it guarantees high security even if a computer is infected with a virus or is observed by third parties. The reason for this is that transfer of bitcoins is impossible without confirmation of it with a USB connection. Additionally, a password and a PIN are required, whereby the credit is protected in case of loss or theft. Should this happen, one can buy a new device and restore all the data with a backup. The most famous device of this type is Trezor.[15]

2.2   Blockchain and Consensus Mechanisms

The blockchain is the heart of bitcoin. It is made up of blocks in which transactions made by miners are centralised. Every 10 minutes a new block is generated that refers to a previous one and this again is related to another previous block. By means of the linked hash values, it can be concluded whether or not the origin is the genesis block, the first block, as only then a block is valid. The block that shows the greatest computational complexity, in the number of completed operations, is the right one since the longest chain lies behind it, and it begins in the genesis block. Thus, the chain with the highest processing capacity grows fastest, and the division can be rectified. Such type of a chain might generate an invalid orphan block. This situation occurs when two blocks are found almost simultaneously. Although orphan blocks are stored in the blockchain, they are not taken into consideration any more. Valid transactions are classified as unverified again and can be added to following blocks that originate in the correct chain. Terminologically speaking, it is called 'the chain forks'. Only if all of the previous transactions and blocks are valid and the origin is the genesis block is the block approved. Additionally, the combined difficulty, i.e. the computational complexity, should be greater than one of the fork.[16]

---

[14] Cf. Ibid, p. 31
[15] Cf. Platzer, 2014, p. 31f
[16] Cf. Mölleken, 2012, p. 31f

The blockchain operates on the principle of distributed accounting. There is no large update as it would take too long and block cash flow. Transactions are separated into small parts instead. In case of a successful search of a solution to a block, the so-called proof-of-work principle is brought into play.[17]

2.2.1 Proof-of-Work

The proof-of-work concept means that all transactions are spread first across the network. Next, the miner picks out transactions that they would like to verify. Generally, these are transactions with high fees. A new block including previous blocks and 4,200 transactions that the miner has chosen should be created. This can be done by solving complex mathematical puzzles through trial and error. Should a miner find a solution, a new block emerges, the included transactions are confirmed and the miner receives the transaction fees as well as the block reward that is used to reward miners for their efforts.[18]

2.2.2 Proof-of-Importance

Another consensus mechanism is the proof-of-importance principle. A person who has been, for example, a part of the system for a long time or is connected with many other participants validates which transaction and whether it is verified. The advantage is that no complex mathematical puzzles should be be solved. It is only checked out if the amount to be sent really exists at the address of the ordering party. It saves a great amount of power, yet it can be easily used by fraudulent people who help one another or by using false cross-linking in order to improve their proof-of-importance score.[19]

2.2.3 Proof-of-Stake

When the right to vote is provided by the size of person's stake and not by their importance, it is called the proof-of-stake consensus. Differently than with the proof-of-importance method, one of the advantages of this mechanism is that coins cannot be counterfeited. It is, however, questionable whether a small group of the wealthy should determine transfer of the money. Transaction fees and block rewards are divided in proportion to the stake respectively. It should be taken into account that the coins used for the vote cannot be spent without decreasing the proportion.[20]

---

[17] Cf. Platzer, 2014, p. 20ff
[18] Cf. Dr.Hosp, 2018, p. 67ff
[19] Cf. Ibid, p. 64f
[20] Cf. Ibid, p. 65

2.3   Transactions

No personal data about counterparties is required for a transaction of cryptocurrency, since the money transfer is conducted just between two people without any intermediary or central entity involved. The advantage of it is the protection of privacy and the fact that payment defaults are impossible due to irrevocable transactions.[21]

There is no data transfer by transactions of bitcoins such as by sending emails as bitcoins are not stored on their own hard disk. With the block reward or by purchasing bitcoins with other currencies, one simply has the right to transfer bitcoins. The available amount is calculated by the addition of the transactions.[22]

A public key of the recipient and a private key of the sender constitute a transaction authentication number (TAN) for a transaction. The key is composed of cryptographic calculations, which is described more precisely in the section 4.2, *Cryptography*.[23]

It works as follows in practice: the recipient sends their public key to the sender, for example, by email. There is no risk in doing so, since the public key can only be used for sending and not for receiving. The sender signs the transaction with using his private key. The transaction is integrated into the next block and, thus, is confirmed and validated.[24]

2.4   The Bitcoin Scalability Problem

Since the number of people using bitcoin is increasing, the current speed of about seven transactions per second is reaching its limit. The speed is low because all users of full node as well as lite clients should run a complete process; therefore, the speed is defined by the slowest nodes. An unwanted side effect is high transaction fees that occur because miners prefer to process more profitable orders. Currently, the size of one block is 1 megabyte. In order for transactions per unit time could to be increased, the memory capacity requirement of one transaction should be reduced, or the size of one block should be increased. Since these changes would empower influential

---

[21] Cf. Wissert, Steffan: Bitcoin Geld ohne Vertrauen in Dritte? Seminar paper. Norderstedt: GRIN Verlag 2013, p.4f
[22] Cf. Mölleken, 2012, p.31f
[23] Cf. Cherek, 2014, p. 20
[24] Cf. Mölleken, 2012, p. 32

participants even more, a suggested increase to 2 or more megabytes has provoked a heated discussion.[25]

2.4.1 Segwit

Segregated Witness, or Segwit, was introduced in 2017 as an update to the transaction format of bitcoin that halves the memory capacity requirement for a transaction. This is feasible as information constituted one part and the signature another part of the overall consumption. The signature has now been integrated into the first half whereby there are 8,400 instead of around 4,200 transactions in one block.[26]

2.4.2 Lightning Network

Different approaches to the scalability problem have resulted in the development of the Lightning Network and other similar off-chain transaction networks. Neither the size or blocks nor the size of transactions is changed here; payments are transferred to so-called payment channels. Only the information that two nodes have created such a channel and have transferred a certain number of bitcoins to it is stored in the blockchain. A transaction between two nodes can be made without the blockchain; it can be conducted by confirmation with their private keys. Thus, any number of transactions can be proceeded. It is possible to close the channel by uploading the account balances with signatures of both partners on the blockchain. Only then does a conventional transaction of the respective balances emerge to their owners.[27]

---

[25] Cf. Dr. Hosp, 2018, p. 87f
[26] Cf. Ibid, p. 89f
[27] Cf. Ibid, p. 101ff

3. History

Bitcoin was not introduced as an ordinary currency launched by a government and it was not established as a company.

David Chaum founded the company DigiCash in 1990 that provided an electronic payment system for the transfer of a small amount of money. Cryptography was used to conduct transactions, and anonymity was of great importance. However, DigiCash was not was met with little response. A digital payment system called e-Gold was launched in 1996. The idea was to combine the safety of gold as well as the major benefits of digital money transfer. One bought precious metals such as gold, silver, palladium and platinum, which were stored in Zurich and London. The value was added to one's account balance. A transaction was conducted through companies, so-called market maker, who sold e-gold as well as exchanged it for other currencies. 2007 the directors of the company were indicted for money laundering, and thus, the company had to be shut down.[28]

All of these motivated Satoshi Nakamoto to develop the bitcoin system.

3.1   Satoshi Nakamoto

Not much is known about Satoshi Nakamoto. All the information comes from his personal P2P foundation profile. The pseudonym indicates himself as male and says he was born on April 5, 1975. He claims that Japan is his homeland; although, it is very unlikely, since he has never written a single word in Japanese. He was 30 years old in the year of the foundation of Bitcoin. It is not known for certain if only one person or a group of people works under the pseudonym. As various qualifications are needed for such a development, it is most likely that a group of computer programmers disguise themselves under the name Satoshi Nakamoto.[29]

On October 31, 2008, he published his paper on Bitcoin under the title 'Bitcoin: A Peer to Peer Electronic Cash System' and the white paper 'A Distributed Time Stamping System for Contracts' on the cryptography mailing list on November 1, 2008. He describes the open source concept, and the operation principle of the new currency is explained explicitly. Moreover, he solves fundamental problems of modern currencies.

---

[28] Cf. Kerscher, Daniel: Bitcoin. Funktionsweise, Risiken und Chancen einer digitalen Währung. 2nd revised and supplemented edition. Dingolfing: Kemacon UG 2014, p. 41ff
[29] Cf. Platzer, 2014, p.189ff

One of the problems is distrust of unknown business partners. Traditional currency systems make us put our trust in governments as well as in central banks. Using bitcoin, one does not have to trust anyone. The problem of distrust is surmounted by safety of the algorithm and validation of the network.[30]

After Bitcoin was launched on January 3, 2009, Nakamoto was working on a further development for 9 months, but then he slowly stepped back until he did not answer any emails and was not online on internet forums.[31]

Many people are trying to find the real Satoshi Nakamoto and wonder why the developer of such an innovation remains anonymous. The main reason lies not in his modesty, but in awareness of the influence of his invention that could change a financial, economic and political balance of power in the world. He might be in danger of being pursued by governments that fear for their authority. Furthermore, the network is based on the principle that everyone has equal rights, and that Bitcoin is developed to meet the requirements of the majority of users and not according to the opinion of the founder. There are many cases of governments pursuing founders of similar systems. Among them are Phil Zimmermann und Dough Jackson.

Phil Zimmermann created a program called PGP that stands for Pretty Good Privacy. The software can be downloaded cost-free. It encrypts emails and other messages using asymmetric cryptography. It means that no third party, such as employers or governments, can read along. Although a legal principle of the secrecy of correspondence applies to emails, the USA and government-related organisations, such as the NSA, violated it. Since this invention would have limited their power, Zimmermann was pursued, and the economic benefit of the program was thwarted. Doug Jackson, CEO of e-Gold, suffered the same fate. As more people used the platform and bypassed the dollar, the US authorities intervened to close the company.[32]

In 2011, the author Joshua Davis was also commissioned by The New Yorker magazine to search for the true identity of Satoshi Nakamoto. Conducting the research, he became aware of Michael Clear, a 23-year-old cryptography student at the time. He replied that even if he were Nakamoto, he would not admit it officially. In 2013

---

[30] Cf. Kerscher, Bitcoin. Funktionsweise, Risiken und Chancen, 2014, p. 41ff
[31] Cf. Platzer, 2014, p. 189ff
[32] Cf, Ibid, p.189ff

Nakamoto's writing style was analysed, according to which the American professor Nick Szabo should hide under the pseudonym. He thanked them for the honour, but denied that he was Nakamoto. In 2014 the magazine Newsweek believed to have found the right person under the pseudonym. Dorian Satoshi Nakamoto, a Californian engineer of Japanese descent. He also denied being the inventor. The next day Nakamoto was briefly online again after four years and announced that he was not Dorian Nakamoto.[33]

3.2 Most Important Events and Share Price Performance

As has already been mentioned, the launch of the first client version took place on January 3, 2009. Satoshi Nakamoto created the first block, the so-called genesis block with the CPU of a normal PC, so the first 50 Bitcoins were distributed. Since there was no reference value for the value of Bitcoin at the beginning, the price was negotiated in a small circle. January 12, 2009 was an important day for Bitcoin, as the first transaction from Satoshi Nakamoto to Hal Dinney with a value of ten Bitcoin took place. The first official exchange rate in the New Liberty Standard was published on 5th October 2009. For one USD you received 1392.33 Bitcoin. The mining difficulty was adapted for the first time on December 30, 2009. The meaning of this is described in the Mining section. A historical event took place on May 5, 2010, Bitcointalk member lazlo bought two pizzas for 10,000 Bitcoin, when at that time the equivalent value was about 25 dollars. At the highest price 10,000 Bitcoin could have been sold for over 180 million dollars. On the 17th of July 2010, the online platform Mt.Gox opened trading with Bitcoin and the exchange in currencies like Dollar, Euro and Yen. This offered a central, easily accessible institution to acquire Bitcoins without mining. The era of GPU mining started on July 18, 2010, when the first block was created with graphics cards and not, as before, with the PC's processor. The only vulnerability of the Bitcoin system so far became known on 15th of August 2010. The protocol rules were broken and thus 184 billion bitcoins could be generated. The error could be fixed by the core developer team within a few hours, the blockchain was forked, and consequently the wrongly generated bitcoins were invalidated. The first mining pool was created on December 16, 2010. Many Bitcoin fans celebrated parity with the dollar on February 9, 2011, i.e. the price equality of the dollar and Bitcoin. The FPGA Mining started on May 20, 2011, which professionalised Bitcoin mining. There was a hacker attack on Mt. Gox in June

---

[33] Cf. Macheck, Alexander: Rebel Yell. Satoshi Nakamoto. In: The Red Bulletin June (2015), p. 26

2011 which triggered a price drop from 31.91 dollars per Bitcoin to 0.01 dollars. On November 28, 2011, the block reward was halved for the first time. Avalod started production of ASIC Mining Riggs on January 31, 2013, which accelerated mining and difficulty increased enormously. The price for Bitcoin exceeded one ounce of silver for the first time on February 15, 2013. The Blockchain forked on March 12, 2013. However, this bug was fixed within a few hours thanks to the international core developer team. The euro crisis led to a rise in the exchange rate to 266 dollars per bitcoin, especially in Cyprus. On November 11, 2013, Bitcoin was ranked by Narrow Money Stock Index among the first 100 currencies in the ranking of currencies, which means that 91 national currencies were behind it. The 29th of November 2013 was one of the most important days in the history of Bitcoin. Due to the high demand in China, it came to a price rise to 1,242 dollars, gold parity was reached, as the gold price per ounce at that time was 1,241.90 dollars. The bankruptcy of Mt Gox in February 2014 triggered a fall in the price to 400 dollars, but this incident attracted a lot of media attention.[34] [35]

More and more companies began to accept Bitcoin, for example Microsoft in December 2014. The last time the price fell below 200 dollars was in January 2015 when Bitstamp was hacked and about 19,000 Bitcoin were stolen. Consequently, the price fluctuated between 200 and 500 dollars until June 2016. The second halving of the block reward to 12.5 Bitcoin took place in the middle of July. Around this time, Bitcoin experienced its first significant upswing since the end of 2013. Within a month, the price rose from 450 to almost 800 dollars. The market calmed down again before Bitcoin broke through the $1,000 mark for the second time in its history on January 3, 2017. The price continued to rise rapidly. Bitcoin Cash split from Bitcoin on the first of August 2017. Not even regulations and the closure of the Bitcoin exchanges in China in the autumn of that year were able to stop this boom. Within a month, the price rose by 300% from 6,500 to 19,500 dollars at the end of the year. At the same time, the CME Group and CBOE Global Markets Inc. also released Bitcoin Futures. Features are described in more detail in chapter 7.2.2, *Futures*. In 2018, prices plummeted, although the currency was being accepted by more and more companies and organisations. There were hardly any new bans or regulations. The main reason for this bear market was, as many people supposed, the unjustifiably high price of almost 20,000 dollars and the

---

[34] Cf. Platzer, 2014, p. 195ff
[35] Cf. Kerscher, Handbuch der digitalen Währungen. 2014, p. 94ff

postponement of the ETF decision of the SEC, the United States Security and Exchanges Commission. ETFs are explained in more detail in section 7.2.1, *ETFs*. The price seemed to have settled at about 6,500 dollars at the end of the year, but then this important level broke, which certainly led to panic sales for many people. As a result, the price fell within a month from $6,400 on November 13, 2018 to $3,300 on December 15. When this text was published, the price was fluctuating between 3,400 and 3,800 dollars.

4. Security

In contrast to traditional currencies and payment systems, a Bitcoin user has his own responsibility for the security of his credit balance. The user must decide which precautions to take or whether the sums involved are too small that do not justify greater effort.

4.1 Anonymity

Anonymity is one of the greatest advantages of Bitcoin compared to conventional currency and payment systems. Since anyone can create addresses without providing any personal data, and so do not contain any information about their own identity, basic anonymity is guaranteed. However, it should be noted that when buying or selling Bitcoin via platforms, proof of identity is usually required in order to prevent fraud.

However, you cannot speak of complete anonymity using Bitcoin since all transactions can be checked in the blockchain. This, combined with the anonymous creation of addresses, creates a pseudo-anonymous character, which creates both transparency and anonymity. Another advantage is that privacy is personally adjustable. This is not possible with conventional financial systems. Cash flows of bank money can always be controlled, which helps law enforcement agencies, but reduces the privacy of innocent people. In the case of cash, it is vice versa.[36]

Improved anonymity can be achieved with two methods. First, it helps to use addresses only for one transaction at a time and to generate a new address for each new payment. This means that it is not so easy to identify a user in the blockchain, but it is possible to calculate which addresses belong to a wallet with not too much computational effort. However, this method poses a problem. Sending Bitcoins is only possible from addresses that have already received payments. For this reason, you either have to transfer bitcoins back and forth between several of your own addresses, which in turn allows conclusions to be drawn about the common user, or you only use addresses that have a so-called unspent input. However, more and more wallets and clients enable transactions to be made from the sum of all addresses. The software automatically transfers the required credit from the various addresses to the destination address. When sending, the entire unspent input is always sent, and the

---

[36] Cf. Platzer, 2014, p. 89ff

change is normally transferred back to the sender address. However, some clients have a function to transfer change to another address.[37]

Another way to cover your financial tracks is Bitcoin mixing which helps to achieve a very high degree of anonymity. There are different types of mixing services, some use less complex strategies, such as the site bitcoinlaundry.com. The service waits until the transfer to the address of the platform has ten confirmations, then it is mixed with others and forwarded to an address chosen by the user. However, it is possible to draw conclusions about the identity of the user by comparing the amounts and charging fees. More complex systems are offered as well. Bitlaundry.com sends the received Bitcoin to different addresses, which are created only for this one purpose. Over the following 3 days, the amount is divided into four transactions and sent to the target wallet at different addresses.[38]

4.2   Cryptography

Cryptography describes encryption and transmission of information. There are different methods of encryption. A method of an asymmetric digital key pair is used for Bitcoin. The digital key pair consists of the public key, which encodes the information, and the private key, which is needed for decryption. This key is kept secret and always remains with the recipient of a message. Moreover, the key serves as a signature as well as proof of identity. It is calculated using hash values. A hash value is calculated with a hash algorithm and is a chain of numbers and letters of a given length. This is unique and forms a hexadecimal string that can be calculated from any input data. A hash value with the same length can be formed from any input quantity. The word 'to hash' is used in IT because its original meaning is 'to chop something into small pieces'. Likewise, the input data is fragmented and then the hash value is calculated from it. It is impossible to deduce the input data from the hash value. Therefore, this calculation is very suitable for passwords, because the password is not stored and compared, which could be read easily in a hacker attack on the website, but rather the hash value, which does not allow one to draw any conclusions. However, the same input data always results in the same hash value, which makes it easy to check. Here is an example for better understanding. Imagine the password being two numbers that add up to one number, for example 3,692. The hash value is 3,692, but you cannot use this

---

[37] Cf. Platzer, p. 93ff
[38] Cf. Ibid, p. 95ff

information to find out which two numbers have been added because there are numerous possibilities. However, you can easily and clearly verify that the hash value is correct if someone tells you that the two numbers were 1,292 and 2,400. This is exactly how cryptography works, only with much more complex calculations.[39] [40]

4.3 Passwords

Passwords are important to ensure security, but you have to make sure that they consist of at least 12 characters. It should contain upper- and lower-case letters, numbers and special characters. Furthermore, it should be noted that the chosen word cannot be found in a dictionary and should not be related to personal data. Obviously, it would be better not to write down the password; although, this is difficult in case of longer passwords without meaning. One should also avoid entering passwords on other PCs.[41]

4.4 Cold Storage

Cold storage is one solution for keeping Bitcoins safely. A digital method is to create a so-called cold wallet, a wallet on a PC that never had and never will have Internet access. Also, it should not be connected to devices that have Internet access. Preferably, the system should be reinstalled and all drivers for WLAN, Bluetooth and other network functions should be uninstalled in order to guarantee 100 percent security. This is a complex method to store Bitcoin, but it offers the highest security. The software can be transferred to the PC and installed there with a USB stick. Although the computer has no internet access, it is possible to transfer Bitcoin to an address generated by it, since this meets all requirements and the network only learns of a new address when a transaction takes place. No one can tell whether this address is offline or not. A client that is well-suited for cold storage is Armory. A full node client is installed on the offline PC and a watch-only client on the online computer. This is used to check its credit; it does not contain a private key, only the imported backup from the offline client. So, you can see your current credit and get money sent to you without storing the keys on an online PC. In order to send bitcoins, a file must be created on the online PC, signed on the offline PC and then sent from the online PC.

---

[39] Cf. Cherek, 2014, p. 17
[40] Cf. Kerscher, Bitcoin. Funktionsweise, Risiken und Chancen, 2014, p. 19ff
[41] Cf. Platzer, 2014, p. 34ff

Although this is complicated, yet it is highly recommended to use this type of storage to everyone who has larger amounts in bitcoin as it is the safest method.[42]

4.4.1 Paper and Mind Wallets

An anlogue method to secure Bitcoin is a so-called mind wallet, i.e. remembering the keys. Another is a paper wallet. It must be noted that the printer does not have a hard disk, otherwise it stores the keys. There is a risk that it can be hacked or stolen. If this is the case, it is better to write down the keys. It should be kept in mind that the analogue or digital memory should be kept safe from environmental influences and theft.[43]

---

[42] Cf. Platzer, 2014, p.77ff
[43] Cf. Ibid, p. 79ff

5. Sources of Bitcoin

There are essentially two ways to get Bitcoins. On the one hand, mining and, on the other hand, exchanging for goods, services or other currencies.

5.1 Mining

Mining is a basic component of the system as without it no transaction would be confirmed and no new bitcoins would be mined.

When mining, transactions are processed and grouped into blocks. On average, a new block is created every 10 minutes and added to the blockchain. Then, this contains all correct transactions that have occurred since the last block. The block contains data from the previous block as well as from the previously included transactions and from new transactions. The addresses of the senders and receivers as well as the amounts can be checked there. For each new block, all previous transactions are validated and confirmed. As a result, you should wait for a few blocks during a transaction to make sure that the transaction has been confirmed and accepted.[44]

In order to prevent a too fast pay-out, the block reward, a reward for processing the transactions and creating a new block, is halved. The event happens about every 4 years. The last reduction took place on 7.09.2016. Once all bitcoins have been created, which estimates put at the year 2140, there will be no more block rewards. After that, miners will be rewarded with transaction fees. This kind of reward already exists. Currently, however, they serve to speed up the transmission and confirmation of a transaction, since the miners prefer to include transactions with a fee in their blocks.[45]

A complex mathematical task must be solved using the proof-of-work, which describes the reward one gets for solving the problem, in order to find a block. The principle is that the key of an algorithm must be found. This is in the form of a hash value and is created from the last transaction. As it has already been described in the chapter 4.2, *Cryptography*, the two summands of the computation must be found. This only functions by trial and error and a lot of computational power is required. Without adjusting the difficulty, the 21 million Bitcoins would soon be mined as hardware developments make ever faster calculations possible, and, with increasing popularity,

---

[44] Cf. Smithers, A.H.: Everything you need to know before buying, selling and investing in Bitcoin. Leipzig: Amazon Distribution GmbH 2013, p. 11
[45] Cf. Mölleken, p. 35ff

more and more people are helping to find a new block. For this reason, there is the adaptation of the difficulty. The level of difficulty is automatically adapted to the available processing capacity of the network. This level of difficulty is adjusted approximately every 2 weeks, exactly every 2016 blocks. The performance of a computer during mining is expressed in hash per second. The units are equal to the processor performance with the subdivisions kilo, mega, giga, tera in steps of a thousand. For example, one Gigahash per second is 1000 Megahashes. In the beginning, people mined using normal PCs. Then, as it became more complex due to increasing difficulty, many used their graphics cards with the GPU because they performed more efficiently. An alternative with lower power consumption was FPGAs, field programmable gate arrays. These highly specialised processors are normally used in research or in industry. Their price, however, was enormous. In 2012, a new invention was introduced to the market, so-called ASICs, application-specific integrated circuit. The AISCs have been specially developed for the algorithms for finding hash values and have enormous performance with low consumption. As solo mining became less and less attractive over time, the era of pool mining began. This describes a group of many miners who search for blocks together. If mining is successful, the reward is divided according to processing power of every miner. It is important to consider who receives the transaction fees and how much of a fee is to be charged for participation. There are also pools that generate not only Bitcoin, but also other cryptocurrencies.[46]

5.2 Trade

There are two ways to obtain Bitcoin, by trade or to exchange it for something else. On the one hand, bitcoin can be accepted as a means of payment for goods or services. On the other hand, you can exchange conventional currencies like Euro or Dollar for Bitcoin. These two methods also work the other way around.

5.2.1 Exchange for Other Currencies

There are different platforms on the internet to buy Bitcoins that work the way an exchange bureau does. For example, the platform called Coinbase is the biggest one in the United States. The most widely used platform in German-speaking countries is bitcoin.de. In contrast to other providers, this platform only moderates the exchange and brings buyers and sellers together. Buyers and sellers can negotiate a price,

---

[46] Cf. Kerscher, Bitcoin. Funktionsweise, Risiken und Chancen, 2014, p.80ff

similar to eBay. As it has already been mentioned, there are some platforms that buy and sell Bitcoin like a classic exchange office. One advantage of it is that any amount can be exchanged; this is often not possible with private exchange, because usually both parties want to sell or buy a certain amount. Another advantage is that the exchanged is carried out immediately. In contrast, for example, at bitcoin.de, you have to wait for a trading partner. Another possibility is offered by the popular website localbitocins.com which mediates buyers and sellers who meet in person and exchange currencies.[47]

The price of Bitcoin is influenced by five criteria that are important for traditional currencies and stocks as well. One of them is the available quantity of money. The number of Bitcoins is limited to 21 million, most of which will have been issued by 2040. As a result, a long-term price increase is expected. Another important point is trust. In the past, it was a crucial factor that had an enormous impact on the course. Once, for example, when the online exchange platform Mt. Gox went bankrupt, the share price plummeted. It should be noted that Bitcoin is not physically backed by gold or other precious metals, so trust, as with fiat currencies, is based on users' belief in the currency. Also, acceptance and dissemination are important, since a new market means new customers and therefore more demand. The security of the currency also has a big impact on the price. For example, once the vulnerability was exploited and many Bitcoins were incorrectly created, the price fell enormously. The last factor is liquidity. If the currency can be bought and sold easily, many people will make use of it. However, if there are only small markets, i.e. too few buyers and sellers, this makes buying as well as selling more difficult and more expensive. This results in a larger spread, the difference between the purchase price and the selling price. The reason for this is that bad offers have to be accepted, otherwise there would be long waiting times.[48]

As a general rule, when owning cryptocurrencies, one should pay attention to whether a capital gains tax on an exchange profit is charged in the country of residence or whether the tax does not apply to it after a certain period of time. Generally, a tax has to be paid on profitable investments such as interest or dividends in cryptocurrencies but not price gains.

---

[47] Cf. Platzer, 2014, p.61ff
[48] Cf. Kerscher, Bitcoin. Funktionsweise, Risiken und Chancen, 2014, p.57ff

5.2.2 Usage as a Means of Payments

Obviously, Bitcoin can be used as a means of payment just like other currencies when selling goods or offering services. However, it should be taken into consideration whether Bitcoin is regarded as currency or a property in the company's headquarters. Usually, this determines whether a sales tax should be paid or not. As laws vary greatly from country to country, it is advisable to consult the competent authorities.

6. Risks and Problems

Since Bitcoin is a new development, many people are not yet aware of the risks of the currency. In many respects, Bitcoin is similar to traditional currencies, but in some aspects, it is more like gold or stocks.

6.1   51% Attack

If an organisation or person in the network has more than 50 percent of the computing power, it or he can attack the system because the rest of the miners would normally reject the incorrect transactions. Now a group of miners has the majority of the computing power and determines which transactions are confirmed and which not. Moreover, they are able to reverse transactions and double-spend coins. With Bitcoin, it is very unlikely that a person will accumulate such an amount of hashing power, as this would be extremely expensive and one would not derive much benefit from it. The only possible scenario would be a pool that crosses the line and is then forced by a third person to launch an attack. In 2013, the BitcoinGuild pool reached the limit of 40 percent; from this point on, no new miners were accepted. Despite this measure and requests from the pool operators to leave the pool in all bitcoin and mining forums, the pool exceeded the limit of 50 percent. In order to double-spend money in a 51% attack, the second payment must be confirmed before the first one. This is can be done easily with 51 % of the computing power, but it also works with less power. It can be achieved by making the first transaction without a transaction fee and the second one with a transaction fee. The second transaction will be confirmed; therefore, the first one will be considered invalid because the money has already been spent. The first transaction pays for something that has been bought, and the second one leads to its own address. As a result, Bitcoins are sent with the valid transaction from one address to another, but the seller thinks that they have received the money.

6.2   Risk of loss

Risk of loss is considered a high risk, as there is no deposit protection or anything similar to this as with savings accounts. For the security already described in the section of the same name, every user is responsible for themselves and nobody assumes liability for loss or theft. Possible reasons for a loss are hardware defects, forgetting or losing the private key or environmental influences on a data storage device such as moisture, fire or a lightning strike. In addition, a data storage device with the internet access can be hacked or spied on and thus the money can go missing.

Stock exchanges and trading platforms are also often targets of hacker attacks, which is why money on such platforms should only be stored for the duration of a purchase or sale.[49]

6.3 Ban

There is a risk that Bitcoin will be banned by a state; although, it is difficult to control whether someone stores Bitcoin at home on their PC, but trading can be banned. This does not harm investors at first, yet the price drops later because Bitcoin can no longer be used as money. Reasons for the ban are that there are the possibilities of illegal, anonymous buying of weapons or drugs as well as the fear that the state currency could lose power. Thailand banned Bitcoin in 2013, but the law was relaxed in 2014. Ecuador and Bolivia also ban Bitcoin because they want to introduce their own digital currency in order to be independent of the dollar. Possession of Bitcoin is also prohibited in Russia, as the rouble is the only legal currency. However, Bitcoin is not very widespread in all these countries; therefore, these bans do not reduce demand significantly. But if Bitcoin were banned in countries such as the US, the UK or Germany, it would probably mean the end of the currency and a loss of capital for Bitcoin owners.[50]

6.4 Regulation

Regulations are normally designed to protect users, but excessive regulations are harmful and constrain the use. The European Banking Supervision Authority (EBA) warned against investing in Bitcoin because of the risk of loss. Germany dealt with Bitcoin relatively early. As early as June 2013, a regulation was brought in according to which speculative income must be taxed. After one year, however, they became tax-free, so the currency was equated with gold. In August 2013, the German Federal Ministry of Finance also declared that Bitcoin is private money and mining is private money creation. These regulations are positive for investors; however, when trading, double taxation occurs which makes the purchase of goods with Bitcoin complicated. In the USA, digital currencies have not been classified as illegal and it has been stated that they have no negative effects. However, the Internal Revenue Service brought in a regulation which has similar advantages for investors as in Germany. Yet it is an obstacle to the purchase of goods as there are 43.4% taxes for a holding period of less

---

[49] Cf. Cherek, 2014, p. 39
[50] Cf. Kerscher, Bitcoin. Funktionsweise, Risiken und Chancen, 2014, p. 100ff

than one year and 23.8% after one year. The Finnish authorities followed the example set by their American colleagues. Regulations were also introduced in China, where many trading platforms are based, and the central bank banned banks from trading Bitcoin.[51]

6.5 Niche Risk

Another danger for the currency is a creation of a niche. This is possible because there are many other digital currencies, since the open source principle allows the software codes to be copied or slightly changed. The first alternative cryptocurrency was the Litecoin. This is only slightly modified and has spread very rapidly. These alternative currencies are called altcoins; currently there are about 600 different ones. A creation of the niche would mean that each group of digital currency users would use its own currency. This prevents rapid spread and makes global acceptance more difficult.[52]

6.6 Control Risk

Imposing controls on Bitcoin is almost impossible due to its decentralisation. After Satoshi Nakamoto pulled back from the development, a small team of developers began to fix security holes and improve the software. Until now, they have always worked in the interest of all users, but there is still the danger that they could influence or manipulate Bitcoin for their own benefit.[53]

6.7 Speculation

Since Bitcoin is a rather small market, speculative bubbles have a very strong effect. This affects the use of Bitcoin as a means of payment, as prices have to be changed continuously, and a price comparison would be very cumbersome. The strongest price movement was in October 2013 when after an all-time high of 1,242 dollars per Bitcoin, the price fell to 400 dollars due to the regulations in China described above.[54]

6.8 The Dangers of Deflation

Since Bitcoin only has a limited number of coins available, deflation is very likely. By 2040, most Bitcoins will have been created. The last coin will be found in 2140. These numbers cannot be changed; however, a sufficient amount of coins is still available because they are divisible to the eighth decimal place that means there will be a total

---

[51] Cf. Kerscher, Bitcoin. Funktionsweise, Risiken und Chancen, 2014, p.109ff
[52] Cf. Ibid, p.114ff
[53] Cf. Cherek, 2014, p.40ff
[54] Cf. Kerscher, Bitcoin. Funktionsweise, Risiken und Chancen, 2014, p.122ff

of 2,100,000,000,000,000,000 so-called satoshis in 2140. A smaller denomination can be introduced. With a normal currency, deflation will cause a fall in prices and, as a result, people will not be interested in making investments because it will be cheaper in the future. This is how the economy of a country decays. Companies lay off employees in order to compensate for their declining sales. This leads to a depression in the affected country. Bitcoin does not exist only in one country; therefore, it is not clear how and whether the foreseeable deflation will affect the global economy.[55]

6.9 Scaling Issues

Scaling is one problem that is growing with increasing popularity of Bitcoin and, as a consequence, could lead to a change to other, more modern cryptocurrencies. In order to replace a traditional means of payment, Bitcoin transactions must not only be secure and decentralised, but also fast and cost-effective. However, this is not the case as there is a limit of seven transfers per second. There are already several solutions such as enlarging the blocks to two or even eight megabytes. Segwit and Lightning are already implemented updates that serve to increase the speed of the network. Both of them have already been described in section 2.4, *The Bitcoin Scalability Problem*.

6.10 Energy Consumption

Since Bitcoin is based on the so-called proof-of-work system and complex calculation operations have to be performed to find blocks, that is, to verify transactions, the energy requirement also goes up with increasing difficulty. This is determined by the computing power in the system and increases with rising prices and an upward distribution because then more miners show interest in processing transactions and receiving block rewards. Other methods of finding consensus in the network, for example proof-of-importance and proof-of-stake, which have been discussed in section 2.2, *Blockchain and Consensus Mechanisms*, are suggested solutions to the problem.[56]

---

[55] Cf. Cherek, 2014, p. 41f
[56] Cf. Dr. Hosp, 2018, p.80

7. Chances and Possible Applications

Bitcoin can offer many opportunities. On the one hand, the system offers possibilities to bypass conventional payment methods; on the other hand, capital gains can be achieved. Bitcoin and the technology behind it have potential.

7.1   Potential Use

Bitcoin can be used not only as a security to achieve capital gains, but it also serves as a cheap, fast and above all unguarded alternative to SEPA credit transfers. In particular, it has great advantages in processing international credit transfers. Goods can be bought with Bitcoin as well. Many online mail-order companies or online service providers such as website designers accept Bitcoin as a means of payment. The apartment rental company 9flats also accepts payment with Bitcoin, and there is a bar called Room77 in Berlin where you can pay for your drinks with the digital currency. Some restaurants and hotels also provide an opportunity to pay with Bitcoin. The donation of Bitcoin is especially handy because micro donations, as for example in crowd founding, are possible. Environmental organisations and the WikiLeaks website also accept donations in the form of Bitcoin.[57]

More and more companies, especially online services, accept cryptocurrencies, including KFC Canada, Reddit and Wikipedia. In addition, Bitcoin is becoming increasingly popular for services where users want to remain anonymous, such as pornography sites. However, since Bitcoin can rarely be used as a means of payment in day-to-day business, Bitpay is trying to bridge the gap between customers who pay with cryptocurrencies and merchants who want to receive fiat money. For a fee, the company accepts the coins and transfers the amount in euros to the seller.[58]

7.2   Increase in Value Potential and Means of Investment

Bitcoin is becoming increasingly important as an investment medium. As a result of the European debt crisis, many people transferred their capital into other currencies. Some invested in Bitcoin, as the currency serves as an excellent value store without state access. The twins Cameron and Tyler Winkle Voss launched their own stock market index representing the value of Bitcoin, with a volume of 20 million dollars and a nominal value of 20 dollars. The Bitcoin Investment Trust BIT of the trading platform

---

[57] Cf. Koller, Christine; Seidl, Markus: Geld war gestern. Wie Bitcoin, Regionalgeld, Zeitbanken und Sharing Economy unser Leben verändern werden. Munich: FinanzBuch Verlag 2014, p.150ff
[58] Cf. Dr.Hosp,2018, p.183ff

operator Barry Silber is a private fund. The conditions for investment are an investment volume of at least 25,000 dollars and an annual income of at least 100,000 dollars, and assets of at least one million dollars are also necessary. Soon, however, the fund is to be converted into a publicly tradable one. These indirect investments are more attractive for people who are less competent with cryptocurrencies.[59]

As already mentioned in section 3.2, *Most Important Events and Share Price Performance*, there are further possibilities to invest in Bitcoin apart from buying them directly and the already described ones. They are called futures and ETFs.

7.2.1 ETFs

Exchange-traded funds follow the price of Bitcoin, but can be traded on conventional stock exchanges. This makes it easier for investors or companies to invest in cryptocurrencies, as they do not have to deal with the functionality or secure storage. So far, however, no ETFs representing the Bitcoin price have been allowed; although, several organisations have tried to have them approved.

7.2.2 Futures

Also, futures allow for people to easily invest in Bitcoin. However, a functional principle is different. So-called futures are contracts in which it is agreed that a Bitcoin is sold to the business partner on a certain day at a certain price. If the price is above the agreed one on the delivery date, the buyer wins because he can immediately sell the cheaply purchased Bitcoin at a profit. However, if the price is lower than the predetermined one, the seller wins, as he can now buy a Bitcoin on the market cheaply and sell this to his partner more expensive. In practice, however, Bitcoin is never really bought, but only the theoretical profit is transferred to the other. Normally, one does not bet on a special price, but only on whether it rises or falls.

If you think that the price would rise, then you are a buyer. This position is called 'long'. You buy Bitcoin at the agreed time at the old price from the betting partner and sell it at the current price. The maximum loss is one hundred percent if Bitcoin reached a value of zero dollars.

If you bet that the price would fall, you are a seller who is said to be short position holder. The seller buys Bitcoin at the agreed time on the market at the current price

---

[59] Cf. Kerscher, Bitcoin. Funktionsweise, Risiken und Chancen, 2014, p.129ff

and sells it to the partner at the old price. The risk is higher as the loss is theoretically unlimited.

7.3 Market Opportunity

Bitcoin's market is growing steadily and, as a result, it reduces the risk of Bitcoin ending up as a niche product. The 15th of November 2012 was an important day for Bitcoin when the website WordPress accepted Bitcoin as a means of payment, since it is the largest hosting site for blogs. Acceptance also increased when the online shop of the American computer retailer Dell accepted Bitcoin. The first products purchased with Bitcoin were alpaca socks in the early 2011. Now you can pay for a wide range of services and goods on the internet with Bitcoin.[60] [61]

7.4 Decentralisation

A significant advantage of Bitcoin is that there are no central banks which often have other objectives such as price stability or supporting the economy. Moreover, Bitcoin is very well protected against attacks and manipulation attempts due to its decentralisation. Also, the decentralisation has other advantages such as anonymity, which has already been described in the chapter 4, *Security*.[62]

7.5 Cost Savings

Bitcoin's transactions are free of charge. Voluntary fees can speed up confirmation, but even these are very low, so traditional providers of transactions such as SEPA credit transfers and credit card payments are not able to keep up with speed or price. Services like PayPal are also more expensive than Bitcoin transfers. If Bitcoin were to be accepted globally by many companies and private individuals, then you could always use Bitcoins for larger or international transfers as they are secure, fast and low-priced.[63]

7.6 Smart Contracts

A blockchain does not only store transactions and verify signatures, as is the case with Bitcoin, but it can also work as a decentralised operating system. Programs can be executed unstoppably and automatically on this operating system. One such application is smart contracts. They allow the immutability, security and

---

[60] Cf. Kerscher, Bitcoin. Funktionsweise, Risiken und Chancen, 2014, p.136ff
[61] Cf. Cherek, 2014, p.43f
[62] Cf. Kerscher, Bitcoin. Funktionsweise, Risiken und Chancen, 2014, p.132ff
[63] Cf. Cherek, 2014, p.44

decentralisation of cryptocurrencies to be integrated into contracts and programs. In order to be able to do this, some kind of permission must be purchased in the form of the cryptocurrency on which the application should be run. Currently, this function is mainly used with the Ethereum Blockchain, which is described in more detail in section 8.3, *Ethereum*. In principle, the Bitcoin blockchain allow such functions as well, but it only knows very simple commands, which is why other blockchains are preferred.[64]

7.7   Tokenisation

Tokenisation is a combination of the cryptocurrency features with ones of real values. For example, fiat money could at the same time exist as tokens or companies could issue shares in tokens. Services or goods can also be represented with the help of tokens, which is usually the case with ICOs. Here the coins often represent some kind of voucher. However, the development is still in its early stage, and it remains to be seen which innovations will come out of it.[65]

7.8   ICOs

Initial coin offerings are newly founded companies that do not raise their capital from investors or banks in the traditional way, but through crowdfunding. In return, private investors receive a token issued by this company, which either represents the product of the company itself or can be redeemed as a voucher for services or products. Of course, these currencies can also be traded, which is why speculation often comes in addition as a reason for such an investment. One example of an ICO is Ethereum. Its currency, Ether, has its own blockchain. Since creating a new blockchain is complicated, these companies generally use ERC20 tokens. A new currency is generated via a smart contract in the Ethereum blockchain.[66]

---

[64] Cf. Dr. Hosp, 2018, p.145f
[65] Cf. Ibid, p.151f
[66] Cf. Ibid, p.189ff

8. Altcoins

Alternative coins are other cryptocurrencies that have more or less adopted large parts of Bitcoin code. Some of them, e.g. Litecoin and Bitcoin Cash, are the result of a fork of the Bitcoin blockchain. Other are based on a whole new code or as ERC20 tokens on Ethereum. It should be noted that the ticker symbol appears in brackets in each of the descriptions. This is a clear abbreviation for the currency so as to avoid confusion, similar to stocks or fiat money. Bitcoin is identified by BTC.

8.1   Litecoin (LTC)

Litecoin represents the first important fork of Bitcoin. In the year 2011, Charlie Lee separated the currency from Bitcoin and introduced some changes. For example, the total number of Litecoin is higher, and new blocks are created every 2.5 minutes. The currency has received much criticism because it was greatly manipulated by its founder. However, this allows fast updates, which is why Litecoin was the first cryptocurrency to introduce Segwit and Lightning Network.[67]

8.2   Bitcoin Cash (BCH)

On 1 August 2017, another important fork occurred in the course of the scaling debate. Bitcoin Cash did not accept Segwit; therefore, the block size was increased to eight megabytes. Apart from that, BCH is very similar to Bitcoin.[68]

8.3   Ethereum (ETH)

Ethereum, the cryptocurrency created by Vitalik Buterin in the year 2013, is based on a completely new idea, i.e. the EVN (Ethereum Virtual Machine). This decentralized operating system allows processing transactions and executing complex operations in the blockchain as discussed in section 7.6, *Smart Contracts*. Ethereum itself was financed by an ICO whereby the token Ether was issued to the investors with which smart contracts can be paid for. Currently, Ethereum is the most widely used cryptocurrency after Bitcoin and also one of the few that has recently used proof-of-stake consensus finding. [69]

---

[67] Cf. Dr. Hosp, 2018, p.143
[68] Cf. Ibid, p.144
[69] Cf. Ibid, p.144ff

8.4   Monero (XMR)

Another category is private coins. They try to increase anonymity and reduce transparency using various methods. Unfortunately, as a result, they do not only protect the privacy of their users, but they are also used by criminal and terrorist organisations. So-called ring signatures are used to anonymise transactions. The transactions are not only signed by the sender, but all transfers occurring in the block are signed by all senders.[70]

8.5   Dash (DASH)

Another method, Dash, uses a mixed algorithm. This means that someone provides coins for a fee with which the tokens that should be sent are mixed. The receiver may then withdraw the number of coins supplied by the sender from the generated pool whereby the information can be transmitted outside the blockchain. On the one hand, the disadvantage is that there is always dependency on a third person and on the other hand this service is fee based.[71]

8.6   Ripple (XRP)

The protocol Ripple and the resulting currency XRP follow another business model. The company of the same name offers banks software solutions based on the Ripple blockchain. This results in broaden scope of the use, which is probably also the reason for XRP's rapid rise to the five most common coins.[72]

8.7   IOTA (MIOTA)

IOTA provides a whole new approach to counteract scaling issues. The users of the currency, not the miner, verify mutually the validity of transactions. Also, not the entire blockchain is stored in each node, but only a series of actions of each node in its 'vicinity'. This system is called Tangle, but since it has not yet been much tested, it is still unclear how resistant it is to manipulation attempts and whether it can ever be used on a large scale.[73]

---

[70] Cf. Ibid, p.152ff
[71] Cf. Ibid, pp.155f
[72] Cf. Ibid, p.159f
[73] Cf. Ibid, p.160f

9. Review

Bitcoin is an interesting innovation in the monetary sector that still has a lot of potential. Currently, it is still difficult and troublesome to use the cryptocurrency as a means of payment, since few people and organisations accept the currency, and the price is volatile. However, Bitcoin would bring many advantages if its distribution increased. The system already shows some advantages. For example, high fees charged by financial service providers in the case of transfer of large amounts or international transactions can be saved, and transactions can be conducted more quickly. Bitcoin is a highly speculative and high-risk investment as can be seen from its past performance. Potential investors should appreciate the above-described risks and acquaint themselves very well with information about Bitcoin. It is even more important to take security precautions seriously, since each user must take responsibility for their own money, and there is no deposit insurance or similar. Blockchain technology looks promising and will revolutionise other sectors if Bitcoin falls short as currency. The possibilities that smart contracts and tokenisation could bring in the future are still difficult to assess, but they certainly offer the potential to turn the current economic system on its head.

Bibliography

Cherek, Oliver: *Bitcoin Risiken und Chancen einer digitalen Währung*. Bachelor thesis. Nordersted: GRIN Verlag 2014

Dr. Hosp, Julian: *Kryptowährungen Bitcoin, Etherium, Blockchain, ICOs & Co. Einfach erklärt*. 2nd edition. Munich: FinanzBuch Verlage 2018

Guttmann, Benjamin: *The Bitcoin Bible. All you need to know about bitcoins*. Norderstedt: BoD - Books on Demand 2013

Kerscher, Daniel: *Bitcoin. Funktionsweise, Risiken und Chancen einer digitalen Währung*. 2nd revised and supplemented edition. Dingolfing: Kemacon UG 2014

Kerscher, Daniel: *Handbuch der digitalen Währungen. Bitcoin, Litecoin und 150 weitere Kryptowährungen im Überblick*. Dingolfing: Kemacon UG 2014

Koller, Christine; Seidl, Markus: *Geld war gestern. Wie Bitcoin, Regionalgeld, Zeitbanken und Sharing Economy unser Leben verändern werden*. Munich: FinanzBuch Verlag 2014

Macheck, Alexander: Rebel Yell. Satoshi Nakamoto. In: The Red Bulletin, June 2015, p.26

Mölleken, Dirk: *Bitcoin Geld ohne Banken – ist das möglich?* Diploma thesis. Hamburg: Diplomica Verlag GmbH 2012

Platzer, Joerg: *Bitcoin kurz & gut. Banking ohne Banken*. Cologne: O'reilly 2014

Smithers, A.H.: *Everything you need to know before buying, selling and investing in Bitcoin*. Leipzig: Amazon Distribution GmbH 2013

Teich, Kai: *Bitcoin Millionäre. Satoshi's Erben packen aus*. Norderstedt: BoD - Books on Demand 2013

Wissert, Steffan: *Bitcoin Geld ohne Vertrauen in Dritte?* Seminar paper. Norderstedt: GRIN Verlag 2013